LEADERS LIKE

PHILIP VERA CRUZ

BY KAREN SU

ILLUSTRATED BY
ARLO LI

Rourke

Before Reading: *Building Background Knowledge and Vocabulary*

Building background knowledge can help children process new information and build upon what they already know. Before reading a book, it is important to tap into what children already know about the topic. This will help them develop their vocabulary and increase their reading comprehension.

Questions and Activities to Build Background Knowledge:

1. Look at the front cover of the book and read the title. What do you think this book will be about?
2. What do you already know about this topic?
3. Take a book walk and skim the pages. Look at the table of contents, photographs, captions, and bold words. Did these text features give you any information or predictions about what you will read in this book?

Vocabulary: *Vocabulary Is Key to Reading Comprehension*

Use the following directions to prompt a conversation about each word.

- Read the vocabulary words.
- What comes to mind when you see each word?
- What do you think each word means?

> ### Vocabulary Words:
> - boycott
> - labor
> - migrant worker
> - oppression
> - organizer
> - strike
> - unions
> - unsung

During Reading: *Reading for Meaning and Understanding*

To achieve deep comprehension of a book, children are encouraged to use close reading strategies. During reading, it is important to have children stop and make connections. These connections result in deeper analysis and understanding of a book.

 Close Reading a Text

During reading, have children stop and talk about the following:

- Any confusing parts
- Any unknown words
- Text to text, text to self, text to world connections
- The main idea in each chapter or heading

Encourage children to use context clues to determine the meaning of any unknown words. These strategies will help children learn to analyze the text more thoroughly as they read.

When you are finished reading this book, turn to the next-to-last page for **Text-Dependent Questions** and an **Extension Activity**.

TABLE OF CONTENTS

FROM THE PHILIPPINES TO DELANO

Have you ever been treated unfairly? Have you ever seen injustice that you wanted to help change? Philip Vera Cruz saw **oppression** firsthand. It made him become a champion for farmworkers' rights.

It was 110 degrees. Philip had worked a 10-hour day under the sun. But he couldn't even relax while eating his dinner. The walls had holes so flies, mosquitoes, and roaches made themselves at home in the kitchen. The showers were outside. The toilet was just a pit in the ground that was too full to use.

Philip thought about his family back home in the Philippines. It would break their hearts to know this was how he and his fellow Filipinos were living in America.

Philip was born on Christmas Day in the Philippines. He worked on farms as a young man. But he wanted to go to school. He went to the US hoping to become a fountain-pen boy. Fountain-pen boys were Filipino students who got scholarships to study in the US and returned to the Philippines for good jobs.

PENSIONADOS

Fountain-pen boys were also called *pensionados*. The US government provided scholarships for Filipino students to study in the US. The goal was for the students to return to the Philippines for government positions.

Philip could only go to school off and on because he had no money. He became a **migrant worker** going wherever he could find a job. In Washington he worked in a box factory, in Chicago as a busboy, in Alaska canning food, and in North Dakota harvesting beets. The longest job he had was as a farmworker in California. Philip worked hard so he could send money home to his family. His brother and sister were able to go to school even if he could not.

ON STRIKE!

In California, Philip picked grapes, lettuce, and asparagus. The growers were very rich, but the farmworkers were paid very little. The farmworkers' living conditions were also terrible. Philip learned that **unions** fought for workers' rights. He joined a union and became an **organizer** in Delano, California where many Filipino Americans worked.

On Sept. 7, 1965, Philip and the rest of the Filipino American farmworkers in the union held a big meeting. They were angry because the growers wanted to lower their wages. They voted to go on **strike**. Philip was one of the 1,500 Filipino American farmworkers who walked off ten fields.

The Filipino American farmworkers asked the Mexican American farmworkers and their union to join them. Together they would make the strike stronger. They agreed! A week later, Mexican American farmworkers walked off another ten fields!

WE WANT EQUALITY

GRAPE COTT

DON'T BUY GRAP

RAPE BOYCOTT
D'T BUY

STAND UP
FOR FARMWORKER

The Filipino and Mexican American farmworkers came together...
... joining their two unions into one...
... the world-famous United Farm Workers (UFW) union.

Their strike inspired people to **boycott** grapes. The Delano Grape Strike lasted five long years. Workers lost pay, housing, and faced many hardships. But they kept going. They made **labor** history. Their strike worked. They got better pay and working conditions.

AWOC
Agricultural Workers
Organizing Co

UNITING TOGETHER!
The historic UFW union was formed when two unions joined together: the largely Filipino American Agriculture Workers Organizing Committee (AWOC) and the largely Mexican American National Farm Workers' Association (NFWA).

U

UNITE

STRIKE

Cesar Chavez became well known as the leader of the UFW. But many did not know Philip Vera Cruz was also an important leader in the union. Many did not know Filipino American farmworkers were the ones who started the historic grape strike. Philip Vera Cruz and other Filipino American leaders were **unsung** heroes.

GRAPE BOYCOTT

NFWA
National Farm
Workers Association

FW
ARM WORKERS

GRAP
BOYCOT

HONORING THE MANONGS

One of the first things Philip and the UFW did after the strike was build Agbayani Village, a retirement home for farmworkers. People from all around the world came to help build it. Philip was in charge of the project. He made sure it met the needs of the *manongs* who lived there. *Manong* is a word given to the elderly Filipino farmworkers who first came to the US.

Many students visited Agbayani Village. Philip loved to talk with them and other visitors, sometimes for hours. He became known as the professor of farmworkers' labor history.

AGBAYANI VILLAGE

A HAVEN

Agbayani Village was where retired farmworkers could live, especially the *manongs*. It honors Paulo Agbayani who died of a heart attack on the picket line during the grape strike.

Philip left the UFW in 1977 but he stayed active in his community. In 1987, he received an award for his long service to Filipinos in the US. Philip was given a trip home to the Philippines to accept the award. It was his first time home since he moved to the US in 1926.

In his retirement, Philip liked to spend time in his garden, take care of his cats, and read. He continued talking about the history of the labor movement until he passed away in 1994.

In Union City, California, the Itliong-Vera Cruz Middle School honors Philip Vera Cruz and fellow Filipino American labor leader Larry Itliong. Philip's letters, notes, and other important papers are kept in the library at Wayne State University. Philip Vera Cruz's story reflects the achievements of the *manongs*. They stood up to the power of the growers and fought for workers' rights.

> **We need the truth more than we need heroes.**
>
> –Philip Vera Cruz

TIME LINE

1904 Philip Vera Cruz is born on December 25 in Saoag, Ilocos Sur, Philippines.

1926 Philip arrives in the US with the dream of going to school.

1942 Philip is drafted into the US military for WWII and sent to Delano for the war effort's food production. Philip joined a union and became an organizer.

1965 The largely Filipino American union membership of the AWOC votes to go on strike.

1965 The Mexican American farmworkers of the NFWA join the strike.

1974 On June 15, over 3,000 people attend the opening of Agbayani Village. In 1978, 21 residents were original strikers. The last of the first generation of retired Filipino American workers who lived there passed away in 1997.

1977 Philip resigns from his position as second vice president of the UFW union.

1987 Philip is awarded the first Ninoy M. Aquino Award for lifetime service to the Filipino community in the US.

1988 Philip returns to the Philippines for the first time since he left in 1926. He meets President Corazon Aquino and his own family members. His life companion Deborah Vollmer goes with him.

1991 The book *Philip Vera Cruz: A Personal History of Filipino Immigrants and the Farmworkers Movement* is published. Philip is invited to speak to students at many colleges and universities teaching the book.

1994 Philip dies in Bakersfield, California on June 12 at Mercy Hospital.

2015 Union City, California officially renames their middle school the Itliong-Vera Cruz Middle School. It's believed to be the first school in the US named after Filipino Americans.

GLOSSARY

boycott (BOI-kaht): to refuse to buy something in order to protest and bring about change

labor (LAY-bur): workers as a group, especially people who do physical work

migrant worker (MYE-gruhnt WUR-ker): a person who moves from place to place to find jobs

oppression (uh-PRES-shuhn): unfair or unjust treatment

organizer (or-GUH-nize-ur): a person who leads a group of people through planning and preparation in order to achieve a goal

strike (strike): a situation where workers stop work in protest in order to force an employer to make changes

unions (YOON-yuhnz): organized groups of workers who help protect workers' rights and improve working conditions

unsung (UHN-sung): lesser known or not celebrated

INDEX

TEXT-DEPENDENT QUESTIONS

1. Why did Philip have to stop going to school in the US?

2. Name at least three different jobs Philip had.

3. How long did the Delano Grape Strike last?

4. What is a boycott?

5. Why are the Filipino American farmworkers and union leaders considered unsung heroes?

EXTENSION ACTIVITY

As you go through one day in your own life, think about the workers who have helped produce the food you eat, clothes you wear, TV you watch, bikes, cars, or buses you ride, books you read, or who teaches you at school. What do you know about different kinds of workers and unions? How can you find out more? What would you be willing to do to support workers who are being treated unfairly?

ABOUT THE AUTHOR

Karen Su teaches Global Asian Studies at the University of Illinois Chicago so that more students can learn about Asian Americans. She remembers her family boycotting grapes during her childhood, but she never learned about the Filipino American farmworkers like Philip Vera Cruz who fought for better pay and working conditions for farmworkers. As a professor, she is a proud member of the UIC United Faculty union at her university.

ABOUT THE ILLUSTRATOR

Arlo Li is an illustrator originally from China and now based in the US. He enjoys creating bright, whimsical, and colorful illustrations and specializes in children's books. He seeks to tell stories through his work and uses tiny details to bring those stories to life. He loves bringing his unique artistic vision to every project he works on.

© 2023 Rourke Educational Media

www.rourkebooks.com

Quote source: Craig Scharlin and Lilia Villanueva. *Philip Vera Cruz: A Personal History of Filipino Immigrants and the Farmworkers Movement.* University of Washington Press, 2002, pp. xxvi and 91.

Edited by: Hailey Scragg
Illustrations by: Arlo Li
Cover and interior layout by: J.J. Giddings

Library of Congress PCN Data

Philip Vera Cruz / Karen Su
(Leaders Like Us)
ISBN 978-1-73165-631-5 (hard cover)
ISBN 978-1-73165-604-9 (soft cover)
ISBN 978-1-73165-613-1 (e-book)
ISBN 978-1-73165-622-3 (e-pub)
Library of Congress Control Number: 2022941353

Rourke Educational Media
Printed in the United States of America
01-0372311937